Hidden Heroes: Kids Who Changed History

Curiosity Chronicles Publishing

Published by Curiosity Chronicles Publishing, 2024.

While every precaution has been taken in the preparation of this book, the publisher assumes no responsibility for errors or omissions, or for damages resulting from the use of the information contained herein.

HIDDEN HEROES: KIDS WHO CHANGED HISTORY

First edition. November 17, 2024.

Copyright © 2024 Curiosity Chronicles Publishing.

ISBN: 979-8230603979

Written by Curiosity Chronicles Publishing.

Hidden Heroes: Kids Who Changed History

Table of Contents

1. The Courage to Stand Up

(1) - 1.1. Meet Claudette Colvin

(2) - 1.2. The Bus Ride That Changed Everything

(3) - 1.3. Igniting a Movement

2. Voices of Protest

(1) - 2.1. The Power of Youth in Activism

(2) - 2.2. The Children's March in Birmingham

(3) - 2.3. The Role of Kids in Movements

3. Breaking Barriers

(1) - 3.1. The Legacy of Ruby Bridges

(2) - 3.2. Facing Desegregation Head-On

(3) - 3.3. The Support Network of Allies

4. The Fight for Equal Education

(1) - 4.1. The Story of Linda Brown

(2) - 4.2. Brown v. Board of Education

(3) - 4.3. Students as Change Agents

5. Young Voices Against War

(1) - 5.1. The Vietnam War and Student Protests

(2) - 5.2. Sally and the Student Activists

(3) - 5.3. Lessons in Civic Engagement

6. Environmental Warriors

(1) - 6.1. The Story of Greta Thunberg

(2) - 6.2. How One Girl Started a Global Movement

(3) - 6.3. Eco-Activism: Young Voices Matter

7. Pioneers of Women's Rights

(1) - 7.1. Meet Malala Yousafzai

(2) - 7.2. The Fight for Girls' Education

(3) - 7.3. Resilience in the Face of Danger

8. Fighting for Disability Rights

(1) - 8.1. The Story of Judy Heumann

(2) - 8.2. The 504 Sit-In: A Turning Point

(3) - 8.3. Empowering Individuals Through Advocacy

9. Cultural Preservation and Change

(1) - 9.1. The Youth Activists of Standing Rock

(2) - 9.2. Protecting Water and Sacred Land

(3) - 9.3. The Power of Community Voices

10. Exploring Racial Justice

(1) - 10.1. The Young Activists of Black Lives Matter

(2) - 10.2. Snapshots of Courage: Youth in Action

(3) - 10.3. Using Social Media to Amplify Voices

11. Addressing Immigration Issues

(1) - 11.1. The Struggles of Young Dreamers

(2) - 11.2. Creating Safe Spaces

(3) - 11.3. Advocacy Through Storytelling

12. The Power of Peer Influence

(1) - 12.1. Leading by Example: Peer Leaders

(2) - 12.2. The Role of Social Circles in Advocacy

(3) - 12.3. Youth-Led Initiatives That Changed Communities

13. Art as Activism

(1) - 13.1. The Impact of Youth Art on Social Change

(2) - 13.2. Using Creativity to Speak Up

(3) - 13.3. Examples of Art in Movements

14. Global Perspectives on Youth Activism

(1) - 14.1. Young Voices in Global Climate Strikes

(2) - 14.2. Activism Across Borders: Connecting Cultures

(3) - 14.3. Empowering Global Change-Makers

15. Your Path to Being a Change Maker

(1) - 15.1. Discovering Your Passion and Purpose

(2) - 15.2. Action Steps: How to Get Involved

(3) - 15.3. Building Your Support Network

1. The Courage to Stand Up

1.1. Meet Claudette Colvin

Claudette Colvin was born on September 5, 1939, in Montgomery, Alabama. Growing up in a segregated South where racial discrimination was everyday life, Claudette witnessed injustice from a young age. She lived with her mother and younger siblings in a neighborhood where the weight of oppression was felt fiercely. Claudette's surroundings taught her early lessons about the unfairness of treating people differently based on their skin color. She was inspired by the stories of powerful figures like her mother, who stood strong against adversity. This sparked a flame of justice in her heart, and she began to recognize that she could challenge these wrongs herself.

Claudette's defining moment came on March 2, 1955, when, at just 15 years old, she refused to give up her seat on a bus to a white woman. In that moment, she wasn't thinking about making history; she was simply tired. Tired of being told she had to give up her rights, tired of the constant discrimination. Her bravery was borne from a sense of deep frustration and injustice. Staring down the bus driver, she stood her ground, knowing that her actions could lead to severe consequences. This extraordinary courage showed that young people can indeed make a significant impact, and that standing up in the face of injustice is a powerful act.

Claudette's stand sparked a wave of change and laid the groundwork for future civil rights activism. Despite facing backlash, she remained steadfast in her beliefs. The strength of her actions is a reminder that courageous choices can inspire others, even if they seem small at the time. Whenever you find yourself facing a challenge or witnessing unfairness, remember Claudette's example. Think about what you might do in her situation, and consider how your actions, no matter how young or small, can contribute to a larger movement for social justice. Every moment provides an opportunity to become a change-maker.

1.2. The Bus Ride That Changed Everything

When 12-year-old Claudette Colvin refused to give up her bus seat on a rainy afternoon in Montgomery, Alabama, she was standing up against years of unfair treatment. It was March 2, 1955, and like many African Americans, she was tired of facing discrimination daily. Claudette had been taught that everyone deserves respect, but as she sat there, she felt a surge of courage. With her heart racing, she refused to get up for a white passenger. In that moment, she made a choice that would resonate through history. She wasn't trying to become famous or to spark a movement; she just wanted to assert her right to sit where she pleased. This act of defiance was not just a simple refusal; it was a powerful statement, and it would soon open up conversations and ignite a flame of change in her community.

The immediate consequences of Claudette's actions were daunting. The bus driver called the police, and she was arrested. As she walked into that police station, Claudette realized she was about to become part of something much bigger. News of her refusal spread quickly, and soon, community leaders and activists began discussing the need to challenge segregation laws. People were inspired to take action and demand change in ways they hadn't considered before. Her bravery prompted discussions about rights, equality, and justice within families and neighborhoods.

Claudette's defiance was a rallying cry, making it clear that young voices, too, could make a difference. She was soon joined by others, and her story laid the groundwork for significant events to come, including the Montgomery Bus Boycott.

Consider this: What would you do in Claudette's shoes? Standing up against unfairness can be terrifying, but every small action counts. Each time you choose to speak up for what is right, you contribute to a larger change. Remember that change is made not just by those who are famous or in power, but also by individuals like Claudette, who chose to take a stand. To keep her legacy alive and be a change-maker today, think about the issues that matter to you. Whether it's bullying in school, environmental concerns, or inequality, there is always something you can do to make your voice heard.

1.3. Igniting a Movement

Claudette Colvin's brave decision to refuse to give up her bus seat was a pivotal moment that contributed profoundly to the Civil Rights Movement. On that fateful day in March 1955, when she was only twelve years old, Claudette did not realize she was making history. Instead, she was standing up against years of systemic racism and the everyday injustices that plagued her community in Montgomery, Alabama. This act sparked conversations about rights and equality at a time when such thoughts were dangerous. Claudette's stand became a catalyst, influencing other activists to take similar risks. What she did signaled to many that change was possible and necessary. Even though her story was overshadowed by others, like Rosa Parks, Claudette was among the first to challenge the status quo, proving that a single act of defiance can ignite a larger movement.

In the wake of her courageous act, young activists began to gather, inspired by Claudette's bravery. These teenagers and young adults, many still in high school, rallied around her cause with a fierce determination to see justice done. Groups like the Youth Council of the NAACP organized meetings and protests, sharing stories of injustice and plotting their next steps. They saw Claudette not just as a symbol but as a sister in the fight for equality. These young activists often faced significant obstacles, from disapproval in their own homes to physical threats from those who opposed their views. Yet, they united and supported one another, demonstrating that youth could be powerful agents of change. Their personal stories of determination and sacrifice remind us that activism knows no age and that standing together can create a force strong enough to break down barriers.

Reflecting on Claudette's impact today shows us how collective action can bring about change. Many young people today continue to strive for justice and equality, drawing on Claudette's example as well as others. They use social media platforms to share information, organize events, and motivate their peers to engage in social justice causes. The movement today is not just about one person or one action; it is about a community of voices coming together to advocate for what is right. Remember, every movement starts with individuals willing to step forward. Your unique voice has the power to inspire change, just like Claudette's did over six decades ago.

2. Voices of Protest

2.1. The Power of Youth in Activism

Young people have always played a vital role in pushing for change throughout history. From the civil rights movement to modern climate activism, youth have been at the forefront, fueled by their passion and sense of justice. For instance, during the 1960s, young activists bravely marched for equality, often risking their safety for the sake of justice. Their desire for a better future motivated them to take action, showing that even in the face of adversity, youth can be powerful agents of change.

When young people organize protests, speak out against injustices, and use their voices to advocate for their beliefs, they show the world that they won't stand by and watch unfairness take place.

One of the most compelling examples of youth activism altering the course of history can be seen in the actions of youth during the 1970s, when they heavily influenced the anti-Vietnam War movement. College campuses became hotbeds of protest, where students spoke out against the war and demanded peace. Their efforts contributed to widespread public dissent, ultimately impacting government decisions and leading to the end of U.S. involvement in Vietnam. Similarly, on a colder day in December 1955, Claudette Colvin was just a teenager when she decided she was tired of being treated unfairly on a segregated bus. Though her actions went largely unnoticed at the time, they laid the groundwork for what would become a monumental movement for civil rights. Each act of defiance, no matter how small, can have a ripple effect.

As you dive deeper into the world of activism, consider what your role might be. What would you do? can be a starting point for discussions among friends about standing up for what is right. Remember that change doesn't always have to come from grand gestures; it can start with small, everyday actions. Carry a notebook to jot down your thoughts on social issues that matter to you. This can help in forming your opinions and planning for action. By examining the successes of youth activists in the past, you can find inspiration and learn that your voice matters. The road may be challenging, but the strength of youth activism has the power to mobilize communities, inspire change, and reshape the future.

2.2. The Children's March in Birmingham

The Children's March in Birmingham was sparked by a yearning for injustice to be corrected. The children involved were inspired by the brave protests of adults fighting for civil rights. They were tired of being treated unfairly, witness to violence, and seeing their families struggle under the weight of discrimination. Many were motivated by their own experiences; 11-year-old Audrey F. knew all too well what it was like to be denied access to places because of the color of her skin. Young participants, often beyond their years in courage, decided it was time to take a stand and make their voices heard. They understood that they could no longer wait for adults to act. By joining the march, they aimed not just to demand change but to uplift their community and show the world that even children could be powerful change agents.

The march's immediate outcome was significant. Images and stories of the children marching, some as young as seven, flooded the nation and grabbed headlines. The brutality they faced, such as fire hoses and police dogs, shocked many people across America. This visual impact propelled the Civil Rights Movement into the national spotlight. The courage of these young activists highlighted the urgent need for change, energizing others and encouraging them to join the fight for equality. By putting their safety on the line, the young marchers inspired missionaries and community allies to step forward, bringing forth both solidarity and additional support to the cause. Events like these propelled real discussions about segregation and civil rights, leading to key legislative actions in the years to follow.

Empowering youth involves recognizing that everyone, regardless of age, has the potential to create meaningful change. The Children's March exemplified this truth in action. Consider how you can make a difference in your community. Whether speaking out against bullying at school or participating in a local community service project, your actions can inspire others. Remember the words of someone who was there: "We had to do something." The marchers' legacy teaches us that taking a stand each day is a critical step in shaping a better world.

2.3. The Role of Kids in Movements

Throughout history, children and teens have played powerful roles in social movements, often igniting change in ways that adults sometimes overlook. A notable example is the youth-led protests that sprang up during the Civil Rights Movement. Young students participated in sit-ins and marches, standing shoulder to shoulder with adults, risking their safety for the future they envisioned. In 1963, the Birmingham Children's Crusade saw young activists endure fire hoses and police dogs, all in their pursuit of equality. Their courage inspired millions and shifted public opinion dramatically, proving that the voices of youth can resonate loudly when they speak out against injustice.

Collective action among youth has been significant throughout history, serving as a bellwether for societal changes. Young people often unite around a common cause, such as climate justice or gun control. The March for Our Lives movement, led by survivors of a school shooting, gathered hundreds of thousands of participants advocating for stricter gun laws. This shows the power of gathering together, as each voice adds weight to the message. When youth rally for a cause, they not only amplify their own messages but also inspire others to join in. History demonstrates that this unity can lead to real, tangible changes, showing that every small step taken together can create monumental shifts in society.

As young change-makers, exploring how to mobilize their peers is crucial. One practical tip is to start conversations about issues they care about, making sure to involve their friends and classmates. Whether it's organizing a school event, participating in community clean-ups, or using social media to raise awareness, every initiative counts. By understanding the power of collective action and recognizing the historical contributions of youth in movements, young people can feel empowered to take initiative and seek change in their communities today.

3. Breaking Barriers

3.1. The Legacy of Ruby Bridges

Ruby Bridges showed incredible bravery when she became the first African American child to integrate an all-white elementary school in New Orleans in 1960. At just six years old, she walked through angry crowds, surrounded by federal marshals, to attend William Frantz Elementary School. This moment was not just remarkable for Ruby; it marked a significant step toward desegregation in schools across the United States. Ruby's actions inspired future generations to fight for equality and justice. As she took her first steps through those school doors, she unknowingly set a foundation for change that many young people would build upon in the following decades. Her bravery reminded us that even the smallest voices can make a powerful impact on the course of history.

The reactions Ruby faced were intense and often hostile. Many people in the community were angered by the idea of a black child integrating their school. Ruby experienced fear and isolation, often being met with shouts and vitriol as she walked to class. Yet, she also received support that showed the beauty of resilience and community. Some families welcomed her and fought alongside her. Teachers like Ms. Barbara Henry became critical allies, standing by Ruby's side and ensuring she received a quality education despite the difficult circumstances. This support highlighted the collective effort required in the fight for civil rights. It wasn't just about one young girl; it was a movement fueled by many who stood with her, understanding that their actions were crucial for progress.

Ruby Bridges' journey teaches us that courage and determination can spark a revolution. In today's world, we can follow her example by standing up for what is right, no matter how difficult it may seem. By advocating for fairness in our schools and communities, we can carry forward Ruby's legacy. Think about what you would do in similar circumstances. Would you have the courage to stand up to injustice? There are many ways to take action, whether it's speaking out against bullying, supporting classmates, or getting involved in social justice initiatives. Each of us has the potential to make a difference, and as Ruby Bridges showed, we can be powerful change agents in our own lives and for the generations to come.

3.2. Facing Desegregation Head-On

In the early 1960s, Ruby Bridges was just six years old when she became a symbol of courage and change. Walking into the all-white William Frantz Elementary School in New Orleans was no small feat. Every day she faced angry crowds, insults, and fear. Ruby was just a child, yet her decision to attend that school challenged the deeply entrenched system of segregation. During that time, many African American children were denied the opportunity to learn alongside their white classmates. Ruby, along with other young pioneers of desegregation, was met with fierce opposition. But she didn't just show up for herself; she opened the door for many others who deserved the same chance at education, courageously stepping forward when so many adults faltered. Her invaluable experience became a catalyst for social change, highlighting the difficulties faced during the desegregation process and inspiring young people everywhere.

Perseverance is a powerful quality that can turn adversity into opportunity. Ruby Bridges, despite her small frame and tender age, illustrated this trait daily. She continued to walk into school, past protests and threats, with the help of her supportive family and U.S.

marshals. This unwavering determination teaches us that facing challenges does not always mean fighting back. Sometimes, the greatest strength lies in simply standing your ground for what is right, even when the world around you is chaotic. It's this spirit of resilience that encourages young activists today. By holding on to hope and taking one step at a time, anyone can become a change-maker. Each story of perseverance, from Ruby's to those of countless others, shows that change might be painfully slow, but it is always possible.

As you reflect on this chapter of history, think about how you can embody the same spirit of perseverance in your own life. Whether in school or at home, challenges will arise. Consider a time when you or someone you knew stood up for something they believed in. What role did support from family and friends play in that experience? Finding allies in your journey can amplify your voice and strengthen your resolve. Just as Ruby did not walk through those school doors alone, you too can build connections that foster change. Remember that every small action counts. Whether you speak out against unfair treatment or support a friend, you are contributing to a larger movement for justice and equality.

3.3. The Support Network of Allies

The courage of young activists like Ruby Bridges was often bolstered by the adults and communities that rallied around them. When Ruby bravely stepped into the all-white William Frantz Elementary School in 1960 as one of the first Black students, she didn't walk alone. Around her stood a dedicated group of guardians, teachers, and community members. They understood that supporting Ruby was not just about her education; it was about challenging the system of segregation that had long oppressed their community. Parents organized themselves, creating a safety net for Ruby that included daily escorts to school, ensuring that she felt secure despite the hostility she faced. This network of support was crucial in helping her stand firm in her beliefs and fight for her right to an education. The combined energy of supportive adults and community advocates demonstrates how crucial it is to have allies—individuals who not only believe in your cause but are also willing to take action to make a difference.

At both local and national levels, influential figures played a key role in assisting youth-led movements. Leaders from various backgrounds recognized the importance of supporting the youth in their quest for justice. For example, educators and civil rights activists often took the time to mentor young people, showing them that their voices mattered. Figures like Malcolm X and Martin Luther King Jr. became symbols of guidance, inspiring youth to advocate for change. Not only did they offer wisdom, but they also helped amplify the messages of young activists. This connection between generations demonstrated that while the youth were leading the charge, they were not alone. Many understood the power of collaboration across ages, paving the way for young people to feel empowered and validated in their fight for equality.

The ongoing struggles for social justice today mirror the efforts made in the past. As you think about the issues that matter to you, consider how you can build your own support network. Whether through mentors, friends, or community groups, having people who share your passion can strengthen your resolve. Look for opportunities to connect with others who advocate for change, and don't shy away from reaching out for help and guidance. Remember, every step you take can pave the way for future generations.

4. The Fight for Equal Education

4.1. The Story of Linda Brown

Linda Brown was a young girl who faced many obstacles in her journey toward education. Growing up in Topeka, Kansas, during the 1950s, she was determined to attend the nearest white school because the only school available to her, a black school, was far away and lacked the resources that the white schools had. Linda's family fought hard for her right to go to school, facing discrimination and prejudice that made their quest for education a challenging battle. Despite their efforts, Linda experienced incidents that made it clear that she and her community were treated as second-class citizens. Her courage to attend school, even when she could not enroll in her local school, showcased her strength and the deep desire for equality that burned in her parents and in her.

Linda's story became a turning point in the fight for educational equality when her father, Oliver Brown, along with other parents, took a stand against the school district. They challenged the segregation laws that kept black children from attending white schools. Their struggle became a landmark case known as Brown v. Board of Education. In 1954, the Supreme Court ruled that segregation in public schools was unconstitutional, marking a vital victory for civil rights and setting the stage for further challenges against racial discrimination in America. Linda's experiences were not just her own; they reflected the broader challenges faced by many African American families in their quest for justice and equality in the education system. Her story inspired many others to stand up against unfair practices and fight for their rights in schools and beyond.

As you think about Linda Brown's journey, consider how her bravery continues to inspire young people today. When faced with injustice, how would you respond? What steps can you take in your school or community to advocate for fairness and equality? Every person has the power to make a difference, just as Linda did with her family and supporters. It's crucial to recognize that even small actions can lead to significant change, so ask yourself: what change do you want to see, and how can you contribute to making that a reality?

4.2. Brown v. Board of Education

The landmark Supreme Court case of Brown v. Board of Education was a turning point in American history, challenging the very foundation of racial segregation in schools. In the early 1950s, African American children were still being denied the right to attend white schools, which were often better funded and equipped. The case was brought by a group of families, including the Brown family in Topeka, Kansas, whose daughter Linda was denied entry to a nearby all-white school. This unfair treatment became a rallying point for change. When the Supreme Court heard the case in 1954, it addressed the question of whether segregating schools based on race violated the Constitution. The Court ultimately decided that "separate but equal" educational facilities were inherently unequal, and thus unconstitutional. This decision changed the landscape of education across the country, as it set a precedent that would challenge segregation in all areas of public life.

The impact of the Brown v. Board of Education decision was profound and sweeping. It not only mandated the desegregation of schools but also inspired countless other civil rights movements. The ruling empowered activists and everyday citizens, making them realize the potential of collective action. Educational policies began to shift, requiring schools to integrate and provide equal opportunities for all students, regardless of race. However, the road to full implementation was not without obstacles. Many schools resisted integration, leading to heated protests and further legal battles. Despite these challenges, the ruling sparked hope and determination in those who fought for justice. It served as a reminder that one decision could ignite a series of changes that would reshape the nation.

Understanding the significance of Brown v. Board of Education encourages today's youth to think about the ways they can make their voices heard. It challenges you to reflect on issues of equality and fairness in your own schools and communities. As you learn about this critical moment in history, consider how you might stand up against injustice, whether it's through awareness campaigns or supportive actions. You can make a positive difference by being informed, speaking out, and advocating for your peers. Remember, every action counts, and often it starts with a simple decision to care and take a stand.

4.3. Students as Change Agents

Throughout history, students have played a crucial role in advocating for educational rights. This activism often arises from a deep sense of injustice and the desire for a better future. For instance, during the Civil Rights Movement, students were at the forefront of protests and sit-ins that challenged segregation laws. They organized rallies, led boycotts, and stood against unfair policies, showing that young voices could create significant change. Often driven by personal experiences of discrimination and inequality, these students highlighted the need for equal access to quality education. The courage of young activists like the Freedom Riders, who risked their safety to promote civil rights, serves as an inspiration, reminding us that age does not limit one's ability to impact the world.

Today, we continue to see remarkable youth initiatives rising across the globe, focused on ensuring equal access to education. A shining example is the March for Our Lives movement, where young people demand not just gun safety, but also advocate for more resources in schools and communities that lack them. Similarly, initiatives like the Global Student Climate Strikes reflect young people's desire to combat environmental issues that directly threaten educational opportunities in many regions. These modern movements demonstrate how students are harnessing their collective power to address complex issues, ultimately creating spaces in which everyone can thrive. By utilizing social media and other platforms, today's youth can unite across borders, amplifying their voices for those who have been silenced.

As you consider the ways you can be a change agent, think about what inspires you the most. What issues do you care about, and how can you use your voice to make a difference? Remember that every small action counts, whether it's speaking up in class, starting a club at your school, or joining local efforts to support education for all. Your ideas and dedication are powerful tools. Finding a community of like-minded peers can amplify your efforts, so look for opportunities to collaborate and brainstorm together. Change is possible, and it often starts with just one student taking a stand.

5. Young Voices Against War

5.1. The Vietnam War and Student Protests

The Vietnam War, which escalated in the 1960s, ignited a firestorm of protest among students across the United States. Many young people felt a deep obligation to speak out against the war, strongly believing it was unjust and unnecessary. The draft, which mandated that young men serve in the military, left students anxious about their future. Many were also influenced by the Civil Rights Movement, which inspired them to advocate for social justice and human rights. They questioned the morality of sending soldiers to fight in a war that seemed far away and was causing extensive suffering. Students organized marches, sit-ins, and rallies, using their voices and energy to challenge the status quo and demand change. They recognized that their generation had the power to shape the future and that their collective action could make a difference.

Among the voices leading this movement were students like Abby Hoffman and Tom Hayden, who spoke passionately at protests and campus gatherings. Their words resonated with thousands who were tired of the violence and destruction associated with the war in Vietnam.

The protests often turned intense, as the opposition towards military action not only brought students together but also created tensions with authority figures. Yet, amidst the chaos, these young advocates found strength in each other. They held meetings in school cafeterias, distributed pamphlets, and found creative ways to express their dissent through art, music, and speeches. This strong, unified front showed the government they could no longer ignore the will of the youth. Thousands of students were determined to fight not just for an end to the war, but for a future they believed in. Their courage and resilience became a source of inspiration, empowering future generations to stand up for their beliefs.

Taking action can be daunting, but every effort counts. Start by learning about current social issues that matter to you, just like those students did decades ago. Join or start discussions about them in your community or school. Social media is a powerful tool that can help spread awareness and connect like-minded individuals. Remember, change often starts small, with conversations and ideas shared among friends. You don't need to plan a large event right away. Just speaking out about what you care about can be a significant first step toward making a difference.

5.2. Sally and the Student Activists

Sally was not just an ordinary teenager; she was a young activist who quickly became a symbol of the anti-war movement in her town. When war broke out and tensions rose, Sally felt a stirring in her heart. She simply couldn't stand by and watch as her friends and family suffered from the consequences of violence. On a sunny Saturday, as she stood in front of a large poster board filled with hand-painted peace symbols, Sally knew this was the moment she had to step up. She gathered her courage and spoke out at a community meeting, sharing her thoughts on why peace was crucial for their future. The room, filled with both adults and young people, grew quiet as they listened to her passionate plea. It was this moment of decision that sparked a fire in many youth around her, leading them to join her cause and organize protests against the war.

Sally's commitment to the anti-war movement inspired her classmates and friends to engage in civic protests. As she spoke about the importance of standing up for their beliefs, others began to see that they could also make a difference. Her friends painted banners with messages of peace, and soon, groups of students began marching together, chanting for change. Across the country, young people were using their voices, just like Sally, standing up against injustice. They organized sit-ins at schools and wrote letters to government officials, advocating for the end of the war. With each protest, Sally realized that their collective voices were powerful. She encouraged her peers to use their creativity, whether through writing songs, making art, or even starting online campaigns. Sally made it clear that change could happen when they acted together, by supporting each other and sharing their ideas.

Every individual action played an important role in the larger movement. As Sally led by example, she also faced challenges, from criticism to the pressure of balancing schoolwork and activism. Yet, the support she found in her community made it all worthwhile. Young activists learned that their efforts were not just about making noise; they were part of a historical wave of change. Sally's journey continues to inspire others today. As you think about the issues that matter to you, remember that every little action counts. If you ever find yourself wondering how you can make a difference, consider talking to friends about a cause you care about, or even organizing a small event at your school. Change often starts with just one person willing to speak up.

5.3. Lessons in Civic Engagement

Being an active citizen is crucial, and history shows us that individual actions can spark significant change. Take the example of the women's suffrage movement in the early 20th century. It was a time when women fought tirelessly for the right to vote. Figures like Susan B. Anthony and Elizabeth Cady Stanton didn't see themselves as heroes; they were just women who believed it was unfair that half the population couldn't participate in democracy. Their courage and determination inspired an entire generation. On the same note, people like Martin Luther King Jr. emerged from the civil rights struggles of the 1950s and 1960s. He often said, "Injustice anywhere is a threat to justice everywhere." His words remind us that being engaged means caring about others, not just oneself. The stories of everyday people standing up against hardships teach us that victory isn't just about grand gestures but also about resilience and commitment to a cause.

These historical lessons shape our understanding of modern activism. The Arab Spring protests highlighted how social media could mobilize individuals across countries, allowing young people to protest against oppressive regimes. This shows us that while the methods may change, the spirit of activism remains the same. Today's activists draw inspiration from those who came before them, realizing that they can influence change in their communities. It's important to recognize that even small actions can create a ripple effect. For instance, when teenagers join community clean-up efforts or start campaigns for mental health awareness at their schools, they are embodying the civic responsibility that has been passed down through generations. The desire to make a difference is increasingly visible in youth-led movements today. The struggles of the past remind us that every voice matters, and together, we can create a more just society.

Consider this: What would you do if you witnessed unfairness or injustice? When you see something happening that you believe is wrong, take a moment to think about how you might respond. Engaging does not always require a grand plan. It might start with a simple question, a conversation with a friend, or sharing information online. Take note of what influences you. Perhaps you are motivated by reading stories of young leaders who fought for causes they believe in. Use their experiences as a toolkit for your own activism. Collect ideas on how to raise awareness of issues that matter to you. Connect with community organizations and see how you can contribute. This is your time to step up and become part of the movement, just as others have done before you.

6. Environmental Warriors

6.1. The Story of Greta Thunberg

Greta Thunberg's journey began when she was just a young student in Sweden. Growing up, she became increasingly aware of the climate crisis and how it affects the planet. At 15, when she learned about the severe impacts of climate change, she decided to take a stand. In August 2018, she started skipping school on Fridays to protest outside the Swedish parliament building, calling for stronger actions on climate change. Her solitary protest soon caught the attention of media and other students, sparking a global movement known as Fridays for Future. Greta's determination and courage spoke to young people everywhere, inspiring them to join her fight for a healthier planet.

Greta's personal story is powerful. She shares how her struggles with anxiety and depression, often exacerbated by the climate crisis, fueled her activism. Many youth resonate with her story because they too feel overwhelmed by the state of the world. Greta's passion and authenticity help bridge the gap between complex scientific issues and the emotional responses they evoke. By talking openly about her experiences, she humanizes the often abstract topic of climate change. Her efforts have sparked worldwide conversations about environmental responsibility, urging individuals of all ages to consider their impact on the planet.

To make a difference like Greta, think about what actions you can take in your own community. Start small by organizing group discussions about climate change at your school or creating awareness campaigns on social media. Every voice matters, and by sharing your thoughts, you could inspire others to follow in your footsteps. Remember, change often starts with one person daring to take a stand.

6.2. How One Girl Started a Global Movement

The School Strike for Climate movement began with one determined girl named Greta Thunberg. At just 15 years old, she felt a deep sense of urgency about climate change when she realized the severe impact it could have on her future. Motivated by a desire for action, Greta decided to skip school and sit outside the Swedish Parliament every Friday, holding a simple sign that read, Skolstrejk för klimatet, which means School Strike for Climate. Her solitary protest caught the attention of people nearby. Soon, photos of her strike spread across social media, and her message began to resonate with others who shared her concerns about the climate crisis. As more young people joined her in the strikes, what started as a small act of defiance grew into a global movement. Millions of students around the world began striking from school to demand stronger action on climate change from their governments. This movement showed how a single voice could inspire a collective demand for change, proving that the courage of one can ignite the passion of many.

As Greta's strike gained momentum, diverse voices joined her call for action, amplifying the message of the movement. Students of all backgrounds, from different countries and cultures, shared their local stories, highlighting how climate change affected their communities. For instance, a young activist from the Philippines spoke about the devastating effects of typhoons in her hometown, while another from India raised awareness about the pollution that made it hard to breathe in the streets. These voices illustrated that climate change isn't just an environmental issue; it's deeply interconnected with social justice, human rights, and economic disparities. Together, these young activists organized marches, held rallies, and shared their stories on social media, creating a wave of enthusiasm that attracted even more supporters. They stood united, acknowledging that they were fighting not just for their own futures but for everyone's future, pushing governments to take immediate and meaningful action.

Through their collective determination, these young activists overcame barriers and made significant strides in raising awareness. They proved that collaboration can lead to tangible results, showing the power of unity in the face of challenges. Supporting each other, they inspired more young people to take part and brought attention to a cause that often gets overshadowed. The movement reminds us that every action counts and that youth voices are incredibly powerful. Each person can make a difference, whether through organizing a local strike, starting conversations in their schools, or simply sharing information online. Engaging in such actions can plant the seeds for broader change, encouraging others to join the quest for a healthier planet.

6.3. Eco-Activism: Young Voices Matter

Young people around the world are stepping up to confront the environmental challenges we face today. From marches and rallies to social media campaigns and community clean-ups, youth activism is taking many forms. Students like Greta Thunberg, who started a global movement by striking from school to demand climate action, inspire others to speak out. In local neighborhoods, groups of kids organize recycling drives or plant trees, showing their commitment to making a difference. These young activists create powerful networks, sharing ideas and encouraging one another to take action. They aren't just talking about problems; they're rolling up their sleeves and working to solve them. This spirit of involvement is not only crucial for raising awareness but also for inspiring their peers and proving that age doesn't limit capability.

Youth-led initiatives have shown impressive results in advocating for policy changes. Whether it's petitioning local governments or presenting ideas at school board meetings, young voices are increasingly heard in the political arena. For example, many high school students have successfully lobbied for more sustainable practices in their schools, like composting and reducing plastic use. They demonstrate that they can influence decision-makers by bringing their issues directly to the forefront. Young activists often grasp the urgency of climate change and integrate their knowledge into their campaigns, bringing fresh perspectives and innovative solutions that engage their communities. This collective action exemplifies how young people can create real change, proving that their voices matter above all else.

Taking action can seem daunting, but every small effort counts. If you're inspired by what you've read, consider starting a project in your school or community. Organize a cleanup at a local park or start a conversation about environmental issues in your class. Connect with like-minded friends and brainstorm ideas that matter to you. Remember that today's young voices are shaping the future, and every step towards a healthier planet is a step worth taking.

7. Pioneers of Women's Rights

7.1. Meet Malala Yousafzai

Malala Yousafzai's journey began in the valley of Swat in Pakistan, a place known for its breathtaking beauty but also its struggles. As a young girl, she was passionate about education and believed that every child deserved the right to learn. At just eleven years old, she began speaking out for girls' education. Inspired by her father, who ran a school, Malala voiced her thoughts and dreams in the face of significant opposition. She even started writing a blog under a pseudonym, revealing her experiences in a world where girls were often discouraged from pursuing schooling. Her words resonated and connected with many, showing the world the importance of education and the power of youth advocacy.

However, her activism came at a high cost. Malala faced immense danger as she openly challenged the Taliban, who had banned girls from attending school. In October 2012, when she was just fifteen, she was targeted and shot in the head by a Taliban gunman. This horrifying act galvanized attention worldwide and highlighted the risks that come with standing up for one's beliefs. Malala's resilience shone through her recovery; instead of retreating from the fight, she emerged stronger. She became an even more powerful advocate for education, traveling globally to speak about the importance of learning for all children, especially girls, demonstrating incredible courage amidst adversity.

People can learn from Malala's story that standing up for what's right can create real change, even in the face of great risk. Reflect on what you would do if you were in her situation. Would you speak out, or would fear hold you back? Think about how you can use your voice to advocate for causes that matter to you. Remember, each small action, like sharing information with friends or standing up for classmates, contributes to a bigger movement. The world needs young leaders, just like Malala, who are not afraid to challenge the status quo and push for a brighter future where education is accessible to all.

7.2. The Fight for Girls' Education

The global struggle for girls' right to education is one filled with passion, bravery, and determination. In many parts of the world, girls face enormous barriers just for seeking an education. Malala Yousafzai, a name that resonates with hope and courage, became a symbol of this fight when she stood up against the Taliban in Pakistan. At just 15 years old, she was targeted for promoting education for girls. Her story, however, didn't end with that attack. Instead, it sparked a worldwide movement to ensure every girl has access to schooling. Malala's bravery not only highlighted the struggles faced by many girls but also inspired countless others to raise their voices for education. She reminds us that one person's fight can ignite change on a global scale.

Education empowers young women in profound ways. When girls are educated, they gain knowledge and skills that allow them to effect real change in their communities. An educated young woman can advocate for herself and others, challenge harmful practices, and contribute to the economy. Statistics show that educated women are more likely to pursue careers, participate in politics, and advocate for equal rights. This ripple effect creates stronger societies and fosters a generation that values equality and justice. Empowerment through education equips girls with the tools they need to navigate and improve their worlds. It's not just about individual success; it's about transforming communities and shaping futures.

Thinking about the fight for girls' education, imagine being in a classroom where everyone around you is encouraged to learn and share ideas. Now, picture a place where girls are told they cannot attend school. This is a reality for many around the world. Consider the power of speaking up, like Malala did, or studying hard to become a role model in communities. You might wonder what you can do. Start by learning more about girls' educational rights and sharing that knowledge. Talk to friends and family about the importance of education for everyone. Become an advocate in your own way, whether by joining a club, writing to decision-makers, or simply spreading awareness. Your actions, no matter how small, can contribute to a bigger change. Every bit of effort counts in the fight for education.

7.3. Resilience in the Face of Danger

Young women around the world face incredible challenges in their pursuit of education. In some countries, cultural norms and economic barriers create significant obstacles. For instance, in regions where child marriage is prevalent, girls are often forced to leave school at a young age, sacrificing their education for the sake of family tradition. In war-torn areas, schools may be destroyed, and the threat of violence makes it dangerous for girls to attend. Even in places where education is available, there may be a lack of resources, such as textbooks or trained teachers, making it hard for young women to succeed. This struggle for education is not just about individual aspirations; it's a fight for basic human rights, and countless young women are courageously pushing back against these forces that seek to hold them down.

Amid these challenges, there are inspiring stories of resilience that shine a light on the power of determination. Take Malala Yousafzai, for example. When she was just 15 years old, she stood up for her right to go to school in Pakistan. Her brave voice and refusal to back down in the face of danger led to her being shot by the Taliban. Yet, instead of silencing her, this tragic event ignited her passion for advocacy on a global scale. Today, she is a symbol of hope and a champion for girls' education worldwide. Another remarkable figure is Wangari Maathai, who not only fought for environmental issues but also emphasized education as a pathway to empowerment for women in Kenya. Her Green Belt Movement focused on planting trees and improving the lives of local communities while inspiring women to take action. These stories remind us that although the road may be rough, resilience can lead to remarkable triumphs.

It's important to think about what actions we can take in our own lives to support young women struggling for education. Consider sharing their stories on social media, participating in campaigns for education rights, or even organizing book drives for schools in underserved areas.

Engaging in conversations about the importance of education can also help raise awareness and promote change in your own community. Every effort counts, no matter how small, and being informed makes each person a crucial part of the solution. The fight for equality and access to education is ongoing, and by standing in solidarity with those facing these challenges, we can contribute to a brighter future for everyone.

8. Fighting for Disability Rights

8.1. The Story of Judy Heumann

Judy Heumann's journey as a disability rights advocate began at a young age. As a child, she contracted polio, which left her unable to walk. This experience shaped her understanding of disability and fueled her passion for advocacy. She was often faced with barriers that restricted her access to education and public spaces, yet Judy refused to accept these limitations. Instead of being discouraged, she became determined to fight for her rights and the rights of others. Her journey wasn't just about her personal struggles but about paving the way for a more inclusive society.

Judy's contributions to the disability rights movement were transformative. One of her most significant achievements was her role in the 504 Sit-in in 1977, where activists occupied a federal building in San Francisco to demand the enforcement of the 504 regulations that would prohibit discrimination against people with disabilities. This action was a pivotal moment in history, bringing national attention to the issues faced by people with disabilities. Through her tireless work, Judy helped to shape policies that changed lives, ensuring that individuals with disabilities could access education, employment, and public services without facing discrimination. Her advocacy not only transformed laws but also changed societal attitudes, inspiring countless individuals to stand up for their rights.

Remember that every small act of advocacy counts. Whether it's educating someone about disability rights or standing up against discrimination in your school, you can make a difference just like Judy Heumann did. Every change starts with one person who is willing to speak up and take action.

8.2. The 504 Sit-In: A Turning Point

The 504 Sit-In in 1977 was a powerful moment in the fight for disability rights. Activists gathered to demand that the government enforce Section 504 of the Rehabilitation Act, which prohibited discrimination against people with disabilities. Many of those involved were people living with disabilities themselves, and their voices filled the hallways with determination and hope. This historic event not only captured the nation's attention but also became a beacon for future generations to rally for their rights. The sit-in lasted for 26 days, setting the stage for the acknowledgment of disability as a pressing civil rights issue.

To demand change and equality, activists employed a variety of strategies during the sit-in. They used the power of nonviolent protest, which included occupying the federal building in San Francisco. Organizers held meetings to strategize and amplify their message, while also crafting clear demands that insisted on action from the government. They drew on the solidarity of their communities, inviting support from various organizations that believed in equal rights for all. They shared personal stories of discrimination and hope, demonstrating to the world that they were not just individuals with disabilities but part of a larger movement for justice and fairness. This approach not only highlighted their struggles but also inspired many others to join the fight for change.

8.3. Empowering Individuals Through Advocacy

Advocacy plays a crucial role in promoting the rights of individuals with disabilities. It sheds light on the challenges they face while pushing for the recognition and respect they deserve. Advocacy allows individuals to tell their stories, making it clear that they are more than just their disabilities. When people speak up for themselves, they demonstrate that their voices matter and that their rights are human rights. Advocacy is not only about identifying problems, but also about working together to find solutions. It involves standing alongside those who need support and empowering them to fight for their rightful place in society. The impact of advocacy can be profound, as it leads to changes in policies, attitudes, and resources that affect millions of lives.

Young people have a powerful role to play in the advocacy movement for change. They can start by educating themselves about the issues faced by individuals with disabilities and sharing that knowledge with their peers. By organizing events or campaigns in schools and communities, they can raise awareness and challenge stereotypes. Volunteering with organizations that focus on disability rights offers young advocates practical experience in supporting those who need it most. Social media is another invaluable tool; by using platforms they already interact with, young people can amplify voices, share stories, and mobilize their friends around important causes. Small actions, such as standing up against bullying or discussing disability rights in a classroom setting, can create ripples of change that inspire others to join the cause.

Encouraging personal involvement is essential. Everyone can be an advocate in their own way, whether it's through writing a letter, creating a poster, or simply starting a conversation about an issue that matters. Those small steps can lead to larger movements and inspire others to act. The first move might feel intimidating, but remember that even the biggest changes begin with a single step. Keeping in touch with local advocacy groups and learning from role models who have made significant impacts can provide guidance and motivation. This journey may have its challenges, but the hope and determination to change lives can lead to a brighter future for everyone.

9. Cultural Preservation and Change

9.1. The Youth Activists of Standing Rock

The young activists at Standing Rock were a powerful force during the fight against the Dakota Access Pipeline. Their journey began when they recognized that their water, their land, and their rights as Indigenous peoples were being threatened. With strong determination in their hearts, these youth stepped up, organizing peaceful protests and bringing together people from all walks of life. They stood together against immense challenges, facing not just physical barriers but also a societal system that often overlooked their voices. Their bravery inspired thousands of allies to join them, amplifying their message of environmental justice.

Through their actions, these young leaders highlighted the importance of protecting Indigenous rights, reminding the world that their heritage and ways of life are deeply connected to the land. They shared stories of their ancestors, traditions, and the sacredness of water, making it clear that this struggle was not just about stopping a pipeline—it was about affirming their identity and ensuring a future for generations to come. Their presence at camps and in media coverage showcased how Indigenous communities could lead the charge for change, urging others to see the intertwined nature of environmental issues and social justice.

Today, the legacy of these youth continues to inspire new activists everywhere. If you find yourself passionate about a cause, remember the courage shown by the young voices at Standing Rock. Organizing efforts, speaking out, and standing in solidarity with others are all ways you can make a difference. Whether it's through starting a conversation in your community or taking action online, every little bit counts in the journey toward justice.

9.2. Protecting Water and Sacred Land

The connection between culture, land, and water rights is deeply rooted in the lives of indigenous peoples around the world. For many, the land is not just a physical space; it is intertwined with their identity, traditions, and spiritual beliefs. Rivers, lakes, and mountains are seen as sacred, embodying the history and stories of their ancestors. Water is essential for life, and access to it often carries significant cultural meaning. When indigenous communities are denied rights to their water and land, it's not just about resources; it is about their very existence and way of life. This relationship has been challenged over the years by outside interests that prioritize profit over people, leading to conflicts over land use and water rights that continue to this day.

Efforts to protect sacred sites have gained momentum globally as awareness of these issues grows. Around the world, indigenous activists and their allies are working tirelessly to safeguard areas that hold spiritual significance and are crucial for cultural practices. For instance, in Australia, the fight to protect sacred rock sites from mining projects has united various indigenous communities. Activism has often taken the form of peaceful protests, legal battles, and community-led initiatives aimed at preserving these important lands for future generations. In places like Standing Rock, North Dakota, Native Americans and supporters gathered to protest the Dakota Access Pipeline, illustrating the power of collective action in defending their rights. These efforts reflect both a deep respect for heritage and a drive to create a better future for the communities involved.

As young advocates, you can connect with these movements by learning about local indigenous issues or organizations that focus on land and water protection. Each voice matters, and sometimes all it takes is raising awareness, whether it's through sharing stories, volunteering your time, or even starting your own projects. Remember, every small action can contribute to a larger change when it comes to protecting our planet and respecting the rights of those who have cared for it for centuries. Engaging with your community and finding ways to uplift indigenous voices can make a profound difference.

9.3. The Power of Community Voices

Community support plays a crucial role in advocacy and cultural preservation. When people come together to support a common cause, their voices become stronger and more resonant. Many stories from history show us that movements have thrived when communities unite to fight for their rights and protect their culture. A perfect example is the fight for civil rights, where neighborhoods stood side by side, advocating for justice and equality. Communities bring individual stories together, creating a powerful narrative that can inspire others and ignite change.

Young activists today are mobilizing their communities in creative and impactful ways. Many use social media to share their messages and connect with like-minded peers. By organizing events, rallies, and meetings, they are not just raising awareness but also building a sense of solidarity among community members. Activists might host workshops to educate their peers about important issues, from climate change to social justice, encouraging everyone to take part. These efforts often resonate beyond their immediate surroundings, as young people's passionate voices attract attention and support from further afield.

Every community has the power to make a difference, and each individual plays an important role in that journey. It's essential to recognize that while young voices are leading the charge, the support of adults and allies can amplify their efforts many times over. Take the time to consider how you might contribute to your community's cause, whether through volunteering, educating yourself on local issues, or simply listening to others. Every small action counts, and together, we can create a mighty chorus that champions important change.

10. Exploring Racial Justice

10.1. The Young Activists of Black Lives Matter

The Black Lives Matter movement began in 2013 after the acquittal of George Zimmerman, who shot and killed Trayvon Martin, an unarmed Black teenager. This moment sparked outrage and motivated many, especially young people, to join the call for justice and equality. Today's youth are using social media, art, and community organizing to make their voices heard. Young activists have become leaders in this movement, speaking out against racism and police violence while also addressing issues like education, housing, and healthcare. They understand that change starts with them and are committed to making a difference.

Many specific campaigns led by young activists have gained national attention. For example, during the 2020 protests against systemic racism, youth groups organized large marches and created powerful messages through murals and online content. They used hashtags like #BlackLivesMatter and #SayHerName to raise awareness about individuals like Breonna Taylor and Sandra Bland, who lost their lives due to police violence. Activism looks different today, with youth engaging in ways that are relevant to them, such as through TikTok challenges or Instagram live discussions. This fresh approach not only highlights their creativity but also fosters a deeper understanding of the complex issues they are tackling.

Young activists are not just looking at the past; they are actively shaping a better future. By sharing their personal stories, they humanize the struggle for justice. Their actions remind us that everyone has the power to make a change. In a world often filled with despair, these young people radiate hope and inspire others to take local actions—whether it's starting a conversation at school or organizing community events. Every effort counts, and each voice adds to the growing chorus demanding justice. Remember, no action is too small to contribute to the larger movement for social justice.

10.2. Snapshots of Courage: Youth in Action

Across history, brave young activists have emerged to confront racism in their communities with powerful stories that resonate through time. Claudette Colvin, at just twelve years old, made a courageous stand when she refused to give up her bus seat to a white woman in Montgomery, Alabama. This happened nine months before Rosa Parks became a household name, but Claudette's act of defiance was born out of frustration with continual unfair treatment. Similarly, in South Africa, young students from Soweto took to the streets in 1976 to protest inferior education, risking their lives for a better future. These youth didn't seek fame or recognition; they simply wanted justice and equality. Their stories are not only inspiring but also serve as powerful reminders that young voices can catalyze change.

Young activists, like those who stood up against racism, used various methods to create awareness and inspire action. Social media became a game-changer, allowing them to share their stories, mobilize supporters, and spread messages quickly. For example, the #BlackLivesMatter movement gained momentum as young people expressed their frustrations and goals through platforms such as Twitter and Instagram, making their voices louder than ever before. In schools, students organized walkouts, created posters, and held discussions, all aimed at challenging racism in their communities. They held teach-ins to educate peers about systemic racism or hosted events to bring diverse groups together, showing that unity is a powerful tool against oppression. Each action, big or small, contributed to a broader wave of change.

Young activists today face both challenges and achievements. While they often struggle against deep-rooted social norms and resistance from authority, their efforts can lead to significant breakthroughs. Many have found support among teachers, family members, and community leaders, highlighting the importance of adult allies in their journey. Engaging in collective action can amplify their impact. They realize that their voices matter and that together they can make a difference. With each step taken towards justice, they pave the path for future generations, proving that courage knows no age. Embracing the spirit of activism starts with understanding one's own power. No action is too small, and every effort counts in the fight against racism. For those inspired to make an impact, think about ways you can stand up for justice in your own community. Whether it's educating yourself, sharing information, or reaching out to others, remember that your voice is important, and your actions can inspire change.

10.3. Using Social Media to Amplify Voices

Social media has changed the way young people get involved in activism and community organizing. In the past, organizing protests or creating awareness about issues often required significant planning and physical gatherings. But with platforms like Twitter, Instagram, and TikTok, one quick post can reach thousands, even millions, in just seconds. Activists can share their stories and ideas directly, without needing traditional media to amplify their message. For many young activists, social media isn't just a tool; it's a lifeline. It creates communities where they can feel connected and empowered to express their views and mobilize others. Youth around the world have used these platforms to highlight injustices and rally support for causes that matter to them. With hashtags and viral challenges, social media gives a creative outlet to their frustrations and hopes, transforming individual experiences into collective movements.

Successful campaigns have emerged from social media, especially in the pursuit of racial justice. One powerful example is the #BlackLivesMatter movement. It began as a response to the acquittal of George Zimmerman in the shooting death of Trayvon Martin in 2013. Initially, it sparked conversations among friends and family, but soon it grew into a worldwide phenomenon that saw thousands of protestors take to the streets demanding justice. Social media played a critical role in sharing stories of those unjustly affected by systemic racism. By using hashtags, people could highlight their experiences, creating a shared narrative that resonated across communities. Similarly, the #SayHerName campaign worked to bring awareness to the stories of Black women who have suffered violence, offering a crucial perspective that often went unheard. These campaigns have not only raised awareness but also sparked real change, challenging institutions to take a stand and address racial inequalities.

Witnessing these movements reminds us that every voice matters. Want to contribute to the conversation? Think about issues you're passionate about. You could start a social media page dedicated to sharing experiences or information. Create content that reflects your values or highlights stories of individuals making a difference. By doing so, you amplify voices that deserve to be heard. Remember that in a digital world, the power to change narratives is at your fingertips.

11. Addressing Immigration Issues

11.1. The Struggles of Young Dreamers

The journey of young immigrants, often referred to as Dreamers, is filled with challenges that can feel overwhelming. Many of these individuals came to the United States as children, brought by their parents in search of better opportunities. They grew up in a land that they love yet often do not have the same legal rights as their peers. Facing the fears of deportation, social stigma, and psychological trauma can be daunting. The struggle to fit in while also navigating a different cultural identity shapes their experiences profoundly. They may feel caught between two worlds—one that they barely remember and another that they call home—leading to a complex sense of belonging. These young dreamers often work hard in school, hoping that education will pave the way to a bright future, yet the persistent uncertainty about their status looms large, making their paths all the more challenging.

The stories of these young dreamers are powerful. Take the story of a young girl named Mariana, who arrived in the U.S. at the age of four. She shares how she would sometimes go to school worried about what could happen if her family was discovered. Legislation surrounding immigration, such as Deferred Action for Childhood Arrivals (DACA), has a significant impact on their lives. For Mariana, DACA provided a reprieve; it allowed her to continue her education and dream about her future without the looming threat of deportation. However, she also describes the anxiety that comes with political uncertainty and the possibility of losing these protections. Many young dreamers like Mariana are not just statistics; they are individuals with dreams, aspirations, and talents waiting to be nurtured. Their resilience is an integral part of their identities, showing us how hope persists even in the face of adversity.

As we reflect on the experiences of young dreamers, it's crucial to understand their fight for a better future is also a collective one. Change comes not only from individual actions but from the support of communities and allies. Each story of struggle brings the potential for action, inspiring others to lend their voice to the cause. Encouraging conversations about immigration policy, volunteering to support local immigrant communities, or simply offering empathy can make a profound difference. Asking ourselves, What would I do in their situation? can help develop a deeper understanding of their struggles. Change can begin from a simple gesture of kindness, creating ripples of support that empower young dreamers to rise above their challenges.

Engaging with these issues not only creates awareness but also helps shaped a society where every dreamer can find their place and thrive.

11.2. Creating Safe Spaces

Safe spaces are crucial for immigrant youths, providing them a refuge where they can express themselves without fear of judgment. Many young immigrants face unique challenges, such as cultural adjustment, language barriers, and the strain of family responsibilities. These pressures can weigh heavily on their mental well-being, often leading to anxiety and isolation. Safe spaces offer these individuals a chance to connect with peers who understand their experiences, fostering a sense of belonging and community. For example, community centers and youth organizations often create programs that allow these young people to share their stories, learn about each other's cultures, and express their feelings in a supportive environment.

Several initiatives have emerged to empower immigrant communities and support their needs. Nonprofit organizations often launch mentorship programs pairing immigrant youths with mentors who provide guidance, share experiences, and help them navigate life's complexities. Additionally, schools are increasingly establishing multicultural clubs where students from various backgrounds can come together. These clubs celebrate diversity and encourage youth to take pride in their heritage while also teaching them how to advocate for themselves and their communities. Local governments and advocacy groups also work tirelessly to ensure that immigrant voices are included in discussions about policies that affect their lives, showcasing the importance of collective action in creating positive change.

Empowering immigrant youth to be advocates for themselves not only benefits their individual growth but also strengthens their communities. By being part of initiatives that celebrate and support their identities, these young people can take pride in who they are and understand the power of their voice. For instance, participating in community service or activism can instill a sense of responsibility and belonging. It's essential for adults and allies to recognize the potential of these youths and provide them the support they need to thrive, ensuring that safe spaces continue to be havens for growth, learning, and empowerment.

11.3. Advocacy Through Storytelling

Storytelling has long been a powerful way to shed light on the struggles faced by immigrants. When you listen to the stories of individuals who have moved across borders in search of a better life, it becomes easier to understand their experiences and the challenges they face. Each story is a piece of history, a slice of life that illustrates both the pain of displacement and the hope that drives these individuals forward. Stories of families separated by borders, children searching for their identity, and communities coming together demonstrate the resilience of the human spirit. Moreover, when these narratives reach a wider audience, they foster empathy and understanding, creating awareness about the rights and needs of immigrants. They remind us all that behind statistics and headlines are real people who deserve dignity and respect.

Connecting our experiences to those of others can spark important conversations that drive change. Sharing stories of personal experiences can help bridge gaps between communities and foster solidarity among those who may not share the same background. Through social media, community events, and all forms of creative expression, young people can become storytellers, sharing their narratives to highlight injustice and advocate for change. Perhaps you've faced a challenge similar to someone else in your community, and by telling your story, you might inspire others to speak up or take action. Creating an environment where voices collide can awaken collective efforts towards justice, allowing them to fuel movements that reflect the passion and hopes of many.

If you want to be an advocate for immigrant rights, remember that your own stories and experiences can be powerful tools for change. Consider how you might share your story or the stories you've heard from others. Is there an event at school where you can present these narratives? Could you write an article for a local publication? Or even start a blog? Every bit of advocacy counts, and your voice matters. Empower others by highlighting shared experiences and challenges, proving that together, change is possible. When you share stories, you remind the world that every individual has a right to be heard, and that awareness is the first step toward meaningful action.

12. The Power of Peer Influence

12.1. Leading by Example: Peer Leaders

Peer leaders play a vital role in inspiring advocacy among youth. These individuals often share experiences that resonate with their peers, making them more relatable than adults. When a young person sees someone like themselves standing up for a cause, it ignites a spark of possibility. For example, think about how a teenager who has experienced bullying may feel empowered when a classmate speaks out against it. It's not just about words; it's about the action and bravery of standing up that resonates deeply. This connection can catalyze others to join in, creating a ripple effect of advocacy that spreads throughout their community.

Across various communities, effective peer-led initiatives offer numerous examples of the power wielded by youth. One compelling instance is a student-run climate action group called Youth for Change, where teens from diverse backgrounds come together to educate their peers about climate issues and organize events like clean-up drives and awareness campaigns. Similar initiatives exist around topics like mental health, bullying prevention, and social justice. In each case, peer leaders not only advocate for their chosen issues but also equip their fellow students with the tools and confidence to speak up. These experiences showcase the ability of youth to enact real change, cementing their role as advocates and leaders.

Recognizing the potential impact of individuals, it's important to note that action doesn't have to be grand to be significant. Starting with small gestures—like choosing to stand up for a friend or initiating conversations about important subjects—can cultivate a strong culture of advocacy. Young people can always look to history for examples. When they see their contemporaries stepping up, it becomes easier to imagine themselves making a difference, too. Remember, every great movement starts with a person willing to take a stand—be that for kindness, justice, or equality. Your involvement matters, and you have the power to inspire change.

12.2. The Role of Social Circles in Advocacy

Social circles can serve as the spark that ignites a flame of change within young people. When friends come together and share their beliefs, it creates an environment where action feels not only possible but necessary. Consider the story of teenagers who rally around a cause, each bringing their energy and passion into a group effort. It's in these moments of unity that motivation surges. Young advocates often draw strength from their peers, gaining confidence to voice their opinions and take action. They might organize a demonstration, create awareness campaigns, or even simply discuss issues during lunch breaks. The encouragement they receive from friends can shift their perceptions, helping them see their potential to make a real impact. This dynamic illustrates how peer influence can turn concerns into movements, making young people feel part of something larger than themselves.

To cultivate positive peer influence in activism, it's essential to foster supportive environments. One effective strategy is empowering young people to share their experiences with social issues, creating a space where others feel inspired to engage. School clubs or community groups can harness this momentum by providing opportunities for collaboration and discussion. By establishing action-oriented projects, everyone involved can see where their contributions fit in the bigger picture. Activities like community service, or even online campaigns, can help reinforce the idea that every effort counts and that change is achievable with collective action. Allies, including teachers and mentors, can play a critical role in guiding young activists while allowing their voices to shine. Acknowledging the diversity of experiences and perspectives adds richness to any advocacy initiative, ultimately motivating more individuals to join in and act together.

Think about how history has shown us the power of social circles. During the civil rights movement, groups of young people often gathered to discuss strategies and support one another in their fight for justice. Moments like these remind us that everyone has something valuable to contribute. Young people should be encouraged to think about their own circles of influence and how they can uplift each other. Creating an open dialogue about social issues can spark new ideas and solutions. Whether it's through art, writing, or public speaking, there are countless ways to express concerns and advocate for change. As you navigate your own journey in advocacy, remember that every action—big or small—serves as a step toward a brighter future. Find your circle, share your passions, and think about what change you can achieve together.

12.3. Youth-Led Initiatives That Changed Communities

Across the globe, young people have risen to the challenge of addressing critical issues in their communities. Initiatives like the "March for Our Lives" movement arose after tragic events, with students advocating for gun control and safety in schools. These young activists organized nationwide protests, showing that their voices matter. In another instance, a group of teenagers in a small town collaborated to create a

HIDDEN HEROES: KIDS WHO CHANGED HISTORY

community garden. This project not only provided fresh produce for families in need but also sparked conversations about healthy eating and environmental stewardship. They didn't just plant seeds in the ground; they planted hope, creating a green space that brought people together and enhanced their neighborhood.

The long-term impacts of these youth-led initiatives stretch far beyond the immediate results. For instance, after their initial protests, "March for Our Lives" continued to influence the political landscape, encouraging young voters to participate and engage with candidates on critical issues. The community garden, initially a small project, expanded into an education program where young people taught their peers and even adults about gardening and nutrition. These transformational experiences help to shift community values, showing adults the importance of including youth in decision-making processes. When young people take action, they inspire others to join them, proving that change is possible and often starts small but can grow into a community movement.

Inspiring youth to take action doesn't have to be overwhelming. Every action counts, no matter how small it may seem. Encouraging students to identify problems they care about in their own schools or neighborhoods can be the first step toward effective change. A simple brainstorming session about issues they face can lead to meaningful projects and initiatives. Workshops that provide tools and strategies make it easier for youth to collaborate, communicate, and lead. Remember, past movements often started with a single act of courage from someone just like you; what will your first step be?

13. Art as Activism

13.1. The Impact of Youth Art on Social Change

Young artists today are becoming powerful voices for change, using their creative talents to shine a light on social issues that matter to them. Through painting, music, dance, and other art forms, these youth are able to express their thoughts and feelings about the world around them. For example, students in a school art program might create murals that depict the challenges faced by their community, such as poverty or discrimination. This not only raises awareness among their peers but also brings attention to these issues in a vibrant and engaging way. By showcasing their art in galleries, social media, or community events, they reach a wider audience and inspire others to think critically about social challenges. The passion and energy behind their work can ignite conversations among their friends and families, making art a bridge between personal experiences and larger social movements.

Art has a unique ability to evoke emotions and inspire people to take action. When young artists create pieces that reflect struggles and triumphs, they don't just tell a story; they invite others to feel something deeply. For instance, a teenage musician may write a song that speaks to the loneliness and isolation felt by many young people today. As others listen, they might find their own feelings mirrored in the lyrics, encouraging them to connect and share their experiences. Historical movements have often been fueled by art, whether it was the songs of the civil rights movement or the murals that filled the streets during protests. In this way, each piece of art becomes a rallying cry for change, reminding us of our shared humanity and the power of collective action. Engaging with art allows individuals to see themselves as part of something greater, motivating them to become active participants in shaping a better future.

Art is not just a reflection of society; it can also be a catalyst for social change. By supporting the creative expressions of young artists, communities can foster an environment where ideas flourish and inspiration grows. Programs that encourage artistic exploration—whether in schools or community centers—provide young people with the tools they need to express their views and advocate for causes they care about. The more young people feel empowered to use their voices, the more likely they are to challenge injustices and push for meaningful reform. As you consider the impact of youth art, think about how you can support the artistic endeavors of those around you. Attend local art shows, share their work on social media, or even create your own art that reflects the world as you see it.

13.2. Using Creativity to Speak Up

Throughout history, people have used creative expressions like music, dance, and visual art to speak out against injustices. For instance, songs have been powerful tools for protest. During the Civil Rights Movement, artists like Billie Holiday and Bob Dylan wrote music that inspired a generation to fight for equality. Their lyrics often reflected the struggles and hopes of those who felt unheard. Murals painted on city walls have also served as a canvas for change, communicating messages of resistance and unity. In neighborhoods around the world, street art has become a voice for the voiceless, allowing communities to express their stories and struggles boldly. These creative forms of protest not only highlight the issues, but they also connect people, sparking dialogue and action.

Art has played a crucial role in influencing social change and policy. One powerful example is the role of graffiti during the Arab Spring. In cities like Cairo, the walls became blank slates for revolutionary messages, calling for freedom and justice. This visual expression brought together thousands of people who felt inspired to join the movement. Another notable instance is the impact of the AIDS Memorial Quilt, which began as a way to honor those lost to the epidemic. Over time, this artwork contributed to increased awareness and policy changes regarding AIDS research and healthcare. These moments remind us that art can challenge the status quo and inspire whole communities to mobilize for change.

When thinking about using creativity for social change, consider how your own passions can play a role. Whether it's writing, painting, dancing, or making music, you have the potential to make an impact. Start by observing the issues that matter to you. Find ways to share your thoughts and feelings through your chosen creative outlet. Get involved in local projects or create something that resonates with your peers. Remember, it only takes one person to ignite change, and your unique voice is powerful.

13.3. Examples of Art in Movements

Art has long been a powerful way to communicate messages and inspire change. For instance, during the civil rights movement, artists used their work to highlight the struggles and aspirations of Black Americans. One famous campaign was the I Am a Man protest in Memphis, where striking sanitation workers boldly displayed signs featuring these words. The artwork behind this message was simple yet profound, evoking the dignity and humanity that the workers demanded. Additionally, the iconic images of marches and protests captured in photographs and paintings helped raise awareness about racial injustice. Artists like Charles White and Jacob Lawrence created pieces that told the stories of people's struggles, reminding viewers that these were not just statistics, but real lives at stake. These artworks fueled the movement's passion and energized supporters, showing how art can elevate voices and create a shared experience around social issues.

Today, many contemporary artists continue this important work, using their platforms to advocate for justice and equality. Artists like Ai Weiwei and Kehinde Wiley have gained international recognition for their activism. Ai Weiwei addresses issues like freedom of speech and human rights through his provocative installations and public art projects. His works often challenge viewers to think critically about the situations surrounding them. Similarly, Kehinde Wiley uses his portraits to rewrite how Black individuals are represented in art history. By placing contemporary Black figures in the same classical poses historically reserved for white subjects, he transforms how we see identity and power. These artists remind us that art is not just for galleries but can be a vital part of social change. Their messages resonate deeply, motivating young people to get involved and make their voices heard.

Consider what you might create to express your own beliefs. Think about how art inspired you or made you feel something powerful. Whether through painting, music, writing, or even digital art, every medium holds the potential to spread messages of change. What would you do if you had the chance to use your art to support a cause you believe in? Experimenting with art can not only be a form of expression but also a way to initiate discussions around issues that matter. So grab a sketchbook, a camera, or even your phone, and start creating. Your voice matters, and your art can be a spark for change.

14. Global Perspectives on Youth Activism

14.1. Young Voices in Global Climate Strikes

The impact of young activists participating in climate strikes can be felt around the world. These passionate students gather in their thousands, waving handmade signs and chanting powerful slogans. Their voices fill parks and streets, urging adults to take action against the climate crisis that threatens their future. Events like the Global Climate Strike, inspired by Greta Thunberg, show how youth can unite to make a difference. It's not just about skipping school; it's about making their demands heard. They are drawing attention to urgent issues like rising sea levels, pollution, and the extinction of species. By taking to the streets, they send a clear message: they want leaders to prioritize the health of the planet. Each march is not just a protest; it's a moment filled with hope, energy, and a strong desire for change. Young people across diverse cultures are creating a wave of momentum that leaders cannot ignore, demonstrating that age does not determine one's power to influence the world.

Key figures leading these strikes come from various backgrounds and have different motivations. Greta Thunberg, for instance, started her journey alone outside the Swedish parliament, driven by fear and a sense of urgency for her future. Her solitary protest ignited a global movement, inspiring many to join her. Other young activists like Malala Yousafzai and Autumn Peltier have also stepped into the spotlight, each bringing their unique stories and experiences to the movement. Malala advocates for education and environmental rights, while Autumn, an Indigenous water protector, passionately fights for clean water and recognizes the deep connection between climate issues and Indigenous rights. They each embody the spirit of advocacy, reminding young activists that they, too, can become leaders in the battle for a sustainable future. Their drive stems from their lived experiences and a shared commitment to educating their peers and communities about the climate crisis.

Every young person can play a role in climate action. Whether it's joining a local strike, starting a conversation with family and friends, or using social media to spread awareness, every action counts. It's crucial to think about what individual talents or passions can contribute to the cause. For those who love art, creating posters for rallies is a perfect way to express concerns. For budding writers, sharing articles or stories about climate issues can help keep the conversation alive. Remember, each small effort adds up; the collective voice of many young individuals can lead to monumental change.

14.2. Activism Across Borders: Connecting Cultures

Youth activists all around the world are finding ways to connect and share their ideas, creating a buzz of inspiration that crosses borders. With the power of technology, these young change-makers exchange strategies through social media, online forums, and video calls. For instance, a student in Brazil can learn from the climate activism strategies of a peer in Sweden, while a teenager in Kenya can share grassroots organizing techniques with someone in the U.S. This exchange of ideas empowers them to tackle local issues with a broader perspective. They realize they are all part of a global movement, united by their passion for change and justice.

Collaborative movements have proven to be powerful in pushing for change. When young people across different countries come together, they can amplify their voices and influence decision-makers on a larger scale. One notable example is the Fridays for Future movement, where students worldwide strike for climate action. This global initiative showcases how collective effort can create significant impact. It not only raises awareness about climate issues but also fosters a sense of solidarity among youth activists. They recognize that while their struggles may differ, they are all fighting for the same future, and together, they can break down barriers and bring about real change.

Change does not happen overnight, and young activists face challenges, including backlash and resistance from those in power. However, even in the face of adversity, they remain hopeful and continue to inspire others. For every setback, there are stories of triumph that shine a light on their resilience. As you explore the world of activism, consider how you can contribute. Whether starting a small initiative in your community or joining with others online, your voice matters. Think about what issues you care about, and take the first step today, because every action counts in the ongoing fight for justice.

14.3. Empowering Global Change-Makers

Numerous organizations work tirelessly to support youth activists across the globe. Groups like Amnesty International and the Global Youth Mobilization focus on empowering young people to advocate for human rights and social change. These organizations provide valuable resources and training, helping youth activists develop the skills they need to take action. For instance, through workshops and mentorship programs, young change-makers learn how to effectively voice their concerns and rally others to their cause. They can connect with peers facing similar struggles, sharing experiences and ideas that ignite passion and determination. Taking a look at grassroots groups like Fridays for Future, which originated from Greta Thunberg's school strike, we see firsthand how one young voice can inspire masses to act. When young people come together, they create powerful movements that demand attention and drive real change.

There are plenty of resources and platforms available for young change-makers eager to make a difference. Websites like Change.org enable them to start petitions on issues they deeply care about, empowering them to gather support and create tangible impact. Social media platforms can also serve as crucial tools for spreading awareness, sharing stories, and mobilizing communities. Young activists can leverage these platforms to reach a global audience, shining a light on their causes and calling for action. Educational websites often provide guides, toolkits, and videos that break down complex issues into understandable information, making it easier for youth to engage. Staying informed about local and global issues through articles, podcasts, and documentaries enhances their knowledge and confidence as change-makers. By engaging with these resources, young people can learn not just about the challenges facing their communities but also about the history of activism and the countless individuals who have fought for justice before them.

Finding ways to take meaningful action starts with understanding personal passions and interests. Young change-makers should consider leveraging their unique talents—whether it's writing, art, or public speaking—to connect with their communities. Every small action counts, and by starting conversations or organizing local events, they can inspire others to join in their efforts. These connections create a supportive network that fosters more significant change. Action and intention go hand in hand, so each step taken, no matter how small, contributes to the broader movement for justice and equality.

15. Your Path to Being a Change Maker

15.1. Discovering Your Passion and Purpose

Understanding your personal interests and values is essential in becoming an effective activist. When you take the time to explore what truly matters to you, you begin to see what issues ignite your passion. This exploration often leads to recognizing what feels unjust or unfair in the world around you. For instance, if you care deeply about the environment, your passion might drive you to join a local clean-up project or advocate for sustainable practices at your school. Clarity about your values can act like a compass, guiding your efforts towards causes that resonate with your convictions and where you feel your voice can make the most impact.

Passions can be powerful catalysts for change, especially for young people. When you identify something you are passionate about, it naturally motivates you to learn more and take action. Maybe it's a particular issue like animal rights, social equality, or education reform that moves you. Understanding your passion creates opportunities for involvement that can shape not only your future but also the lives of those around you. For example, consider people like Malala Yousafzai, who, driven by her love for education and equality, became a powerful voice against oppression. Her journey teaches us that individual passions, combined with courage, can lead to monumental changes.

As you reflect on your interests, think of this as an ongoing journey rather than a specific destination. It is essential to remember the impact you can have, no matter how small your steps may seem. Engage with others who share your passions and encourage friends to also explore what moves them. Always ask yourself, "What can I do today to help create positive change?" Each choice you make can add up to significant outcomes for your community and the world. So, take a moment to jot down what brings you joy and what issues you care about most; this can be the first step toward discovering your purpose and making a difference.

15.2. Action Steps: How to Get Involved

Getting involved in social justice and advocacy starts with understanding that your voice matters. You can take practical steps, like joining local organizations that focus on issues you care about, such as education equity or environmental justice. Many groups welcome young members and have programs designed to empower youth. Participating in community events, whether they're marches, workshops, or volunteer days, can also help you connect with like-minded individuals who are passionate about change. Engaging in discussions about social issues in your school or online can spark important conversations and encourage others to join you in advocacy.

Participation in activism can take many forms, ranging from something as local as organizing a fundraiser for a community cause to something global, such as using social media to raise awareness about issues affecting people around the world. You might choose to write letters to your government representatives about policies you believe in, or you could even start a petition for your school to adopt more inclusive practices. Each act, no matter how small, contributes to a larger movement for change. The beauty of activism is that it's not limited to one way of participating; every effort counts, whether it's online, in your community, or on a national scale.

To keep yourself motivated, think about the impact you want to make and let that guide your actions. Consider the stories of young activists from the past and how their decisions shaped our world today. You have the chance to create change now, and it begins with taking those first steps. Remember that change often starts with a simple question: What can I do? So, write down those thoughts, and find ways in your community to turn them into action. Whether it's starting a blog, volunteering your time, or simply being a friend to someone in need, these businesses can help you make a difference and inspire others along the way. Your journey in advocacy could be just beginning, but the potential for impact is truly limitless.

15.3. Building Your Support Network

Creating a network of allies is essential for anyone looking to advocate for change. This network can be made up of friends, family members, teachers, and community leaders who share your passion for social justice. When you start building this network, think about the people in your life who support your ideas, no matter how big or small. They can help amplify your voice and provide guidance when challenges arise. For example, when young activists like Malala Yousafzai were fighting for girls' education, they didn't do it alone. They found mentors who believed in their mission, and together they worked to create a bigger impact. Start by discussing your advocacy goals with those who already support you; they might have valuable insights or connections that could strengthen your efforts.

Value lies in collaboration and teamwork. When diverse individuals come together, they bring unique perspectives that can lead to innovative solutions. For instance, groups like the Civil Rights Movement united people from different backgrounds to fight against injustice. Each person's unique experience contributed to a broader understanding of the issues at hand. You don't have to face your advocacy journey alone; teamwork allows you to share the workload and celebrate successes together. Remember, every small achievement can create ripple effects, encouraging others to hop on board. Whether organizing a local event or spreading awareness on social media, working alongside others can make your efforts more impactful while fostering friendship and community spirit.

Think about ways you can build your support network today. Reach out to someone you admire and ask how they got involved in advocacy. Set a goal to connect with at least one new person each week who shares your interests. By nurturing these relationships, you'll find a sense of belonging that can propel your advocacy forward. Surrounding yourself with supportive people will help you navigate the ups and downs you might face. Together, you can cultivate a community focused on making a difference, providing both encouragement and motivation. Your journey toward change can be strengthened when you embrace the power of collective action.

Milton Keynes UK
Ingram Content Group UK Ltd.
UKHW020915291124
451807UK00013B/932